Henry Augustus Rawes

Cui Bono?

University Education. A Letter to a Catholic Layman

Henry Augustus Rawes

Cui Bono?
University Education. A Letter to a Catholic Layman

ISBN/EAN: 9783337798826

Printed in Europe, USA, Canada, Australia, Japan

Cover: Foto ©Thomas Meinert / pixelio.de

More available books at **www.hansebooks.com**

CUI BONO?

UNIVERSITY EDUCATION.

A LETTER

TO

A CATHOLIC LAYMAN,

BY

THE REV. H. A. RAWES, M. A.

OF TRINITY COLLEGE, CAMBRIDGE;

Priest of the Congregation of the Oblates of St. Charles.

THUS SAITH THE LORD; STAND YE ON THE WAYS AND SEE AND ASK FOR THE OLD PATHS, WHICH IS THE GOOD WAY, AND WALK YE IN IT: AND YE SHALL FIND REFRESHMENT FOR YOUR SOULS. JER. vi. 16.

LONDON:
LONGMAN, GREEN, LONGMAN, ROBERTS, AND GREEN.
W. KNOWLES, 7, NORFOLK ROAD, BAYSWATER.
DUBLIN: J. DUFFY, WELLINGTON QUAY.
1864.

PRINTED BY
W. KNOWLES, 7, NORFOLK ROAD, BAYSWATER.

SIR,

I do not know in the least to whom I am addressing this letter. It may be to a person whom I know, to one whom I know by name, or to one about whom I know nothing. However as you have printed and published your views on University Education, you can not possibly make any objection to receiving a letter on that subject from me or from any one else. I have only just seen your letter, though it may have been published for some little time. Now I will begin by saying that I never remember having read a Catholic Letter or Pamphlet from which I differ so utterly, on almost all points, as from yours. I differ from you as to your conclusions; I differ from you as to very many of your opinions; and I differ from you, in the widest possible manner, as to the principle which underlies this scheme. For I look upon this proposition of sending young Catholics to Oxford or Cambridge, as only one of those many developments or signs, which we see everywhere around us, of that spirit of worldliness which is coming in on the Church. I will explain what I mean further on. Here I will only say that

A

I neither make nor intend to make any accusation against you personally; I am speaking only of your proposal. I may call it yours; as you have by adoption made it your own. And you cannot be offended at me for saying how much I dislike it, because having published your Letter you invite comment; and moreover I hold you at perfect liberty to say what you like about me. I am not thin-skinned in these matters. I think that your Letter is most mischievous in its tendencies and therefore I say so. I believe it to be contrary to the instinct of the faithful, contrary to the sense of the Priesthood in this land, and contrary to a true spirit of loyalty to the Church. But I do not say that you are consciously wanting in that spirit of loyalty. I do not mean either to say this or to insinuate it. If you choose to say that I am narrow-minded or puritanical or behind the times, and so on, I shall not complain. You have a right to your opinions and I have a right to mine. You have a right to say what you think of my views and I have a right to say what I think of yours. And charity will not suffer by this.

The first thing that you must do is to prove the greatness of the want which is said to exist as regards University Education for Catholic youth. You say, "I start from the admitted fact that some University Education is indispensable for Catholic youth." I grant you that, if you substitute "very desirable" for "indispensable." I know of nothing that is indispensable for Catholic youths, except the faith and morals of the Church. But are there sufficient numbers of Catholic youths seeking for this Education, to make it possible to give it to them at once? I do not know in the least whether there be or not; but it could be easily ascertained. Your own statement goes far to prove that this want is much exaggerated. For you say that in the last few years only twenty Catholic Students have passed through Oxford. This does not seem to speak of any great want. Still you might fairly say that this only represents the number of those persons who have not been afraid of putting the faith of their children in peril, for some fancied worldly advantage: whereas multitudes of others, desirous of the same advantages for their children, have not ventured on this.

But, if there are as many as we are led to suppose, it seems that a University such as that proposed by the writer, whom you are answering, might at once be started with every prospect of success. And if they are not so numerous, but are only few in number, why, they must accept the necessities of their position and be content with what they have. The Church is the best judge of what is necessary or advantageous for her children. And (to anticipate what I shall say afterwards) there is, in Dublin, a Catholic University for those who speak the English tongue. I put this forward only as a temporary arrangement, for I think that the right thing in the right place is a Catholic University in England. But a University cannot be built in a day; and if it has pleased God that we should belong to a Church, which for so long in this land has been trodden down and persecuted, and which is only now emerging from penal laws and social persecution, we must take one thing with another and be thankful; and not grumble if there are a few knots in the rope as it slips through our hands.　Most of us who have had the priceless blessing of a conversion to the Faith have suffered more or less in our worldly prospects, but I have never heard any one complain of this; indeed I may say truly that I have never known any one so mean-spirited as to feel it.　And why should any expect to have every thing just as they like in this matter of Education?　You say that you know of "many parents" who "intend to send their sons to Protestant Colleges if a Catholic College be not soon founded."　Well, that is their look out.　If they so far forget their duty to God and their children and their own consciences, they will have to settle the matter one day with their Judge.　Their doing it will not make it right; and if the Church does all that she can for them, she will not be to blame.　The Church always does that which is best in the highest sense for her children; but she is never led by the whims and fancies of the many, still less of the few.　It is simply unreasonable to expect that everything can be done in a moment.　As you know of these persons and their intention, the best thing you can do is to warn them, if you have an opportunity, against carrying their intentions into effect.

You might know of a burglar who intended to break into the house of one of your friends, unless he sent him a twenty-pound note : but you would not, I suppose, recommend your friend to send it. But what makes this case, of which I am speaking, worse, is that you have said in another place : " those Catholic parents who have done so, would perhaps be as little disposed as any one to defend on principle what they have done under peculiar circumstances." Did you correct the proof of your letter ? Or has this sentence got in somehow when you never wrote it ? Are men who can act like this to be brought forward as examples or arguments ? Surely this is doing evil that evil may come; or at most that some supposed worldly advantage may come. The next time I hear of a man committing forgery I shall say : ' He who has done so would perhaps be as little disposed as any one to defend on principle what he has done under the influence of peculiar circumstances.' What should you think of my moralizing in this case ?

Let me now briefly glance at the only ways in which this question can be met. And the question I observe is now about a University Education, not at all about using a University as an examining Board, (this you have yourself said) as for instance, the University of London. To that there does not seem to be, as far as I know, any objection : at any rate whether there be or not, that is not now the question in dispute. For my own part I should think it better not to be dependent on Protestants even for this.

1. You may send young men to Protestant Universities.

2. You may have a Catholic College, in a Protestant University.

3. You may have an English University in Rome ; or you may go to some of the foreign Universities.

4. You may have an English University in England.

5. You may go to the Catholic University in Dublin.

1. All persons, I believe, (including those parents who under "peculiar circumstances" have done what they thought wrong) consider the first plan to be altogether indefensible in theory and very dangerous in practice.

2. As to the second plan : I can imagine no more pitiable spectacle than for the members of the great Catholic Commonwealth to be standing, with their hats in their hands, begging for Educational alms at the doors of the Protestant Universities :

" Pity the sorrows of a poor old man,
Whose trembling limbs have borne him to your door."

We are thus invited to "beg or borrow" our education; it does not matter which. I dislike, as much as I can, this begging or borrowing proposal.

My object now is not to state the arguments for it or against it. They are to be found in your Letter and the Review of which you speak. It is of no use going over that ground again. But I wish to point out a few places in which your argument entirely fails : and I wish also to enter my protest, as strongly as I can, against your proposal. I am not going to sit quiet and say nothing when so monstrous a proposition is made.

And indeed there is at present no need of going into details for as you say truly, the plan which you "advocate is not yet a possible one." You are only "arguing against those Catholics who wish to prevent it becoming ever possible." I am one of those Catholics. I shall always do whatever little I can to prevent the realization of such a plan. I shall always contend against it, tooth and nail. And I feel certain that it never will be possible: first because the Universities will never agree to it; next, because our Bishops will never sanction it; thirdly, because the Holy See will never permit it. Using partly your own words, I say that "my faith in the wisdom of the Church is too strong to allow me to fear that she will ever" suffer such a plan to be possible.

And what is the good of this plan? What is the advantage you propose to seek? This is the kernel of the matter. Is the good, thus supposed to be within our reach, spiritual, moral, intellectual, or worldly? It is neither spiritual nor moral because your plan literally bristles with precautions against moral and spiritual dangers. You yourself say that the greatest precautions must be used against these dangers. I, with multitudes of others, believe that all these precautions will be unable to avert the danger, or even to mitigate it to any appreciable extent. Is it intellectual good? No, it can not be that. Every one is agreed that the ordinary University Lectures are not in any way remarkable for ability: that there is in fact nothing in them which can not easily be got elsewhere. The advantage therefore is merely a fancied worldly advantage. I see plainly what you mean. There is supposed to be a social prestige belonging to those who have been at Oxford or Cambridge. It may exist; I think it does exist, but I am sure that it is decreasing every year. By the time that a few hundred Catholics are sacrificed at its shrine, it will most likely be gone for ever. There is another reason which shows that this is your drift. You never mention Durham. But from what I know about it, I am certain that the Education there is in every way equal to that at Oxford or Cambridge. I remember some twelve years ago that most Anglican Bishops were said to prefer candidates for ordination from Durham to those from the two great Universities. But as to social prestige Durham does not rank with them. Consequently it is out of the question. Are you, then, prepared to risk souls for such a miserable paltry gain as this? I look upon this proposition as the outcoming (I believe the unconscious outcoming) of that spirit of worldliness which is now surrounding us with such terrible dangers. Now that is what I think, and I must say it : though I would not willingly and unnecessarily cause pain to you or any one else. Is it coming to this that we are to be ashamed of the reproach of the Cross ? Do we expect in every way to have this world as well as the next ? Is the Church expected to sanction a plan full of perils for souls, in order that this person or that may say he has been to Oxford or Cambridge, as the case may be ? Believe me this will never be. I pass by the 3rd and 4th plans, only remarking that my own personal feelings are strongly in favor of a Catholic University in some central part of England ; and that my firm conviction is that it could be carried out successfully, if not at once, yet shortly and by degrees. I pass by these two plans, because the main arguments for and against the 4th are to be found in the Review of which you are speaking, and every one can judge for himself : and as to the 3rd it has never in any way, that I know of, been brought prominently forward.

So I come to the 5th plan, and I ask these persons who are so anxious for a University Education, before the Church in this land has had time to turn herself round, why do they not go to Dublin ? Say it is only a provisional arrangement ; why do they not go there till something can be done in England ? Dublin is a University founded by the Holy See ; this is its sanction ; it could have none higher. And in that University are to be found as able Professors as you can find in the Three Kingdoms. Any one must know this who has read their contributions to the Atlantis, which was one of the most brilliant and masterly Periodicals ever published. One great name indeed is there no longer : and one most accomplished scholar has been taken from this world : but as a whole that University is worthily doing its work, and they who are left are following in the footsteps of those who are gone. Why then can not our youth go *for the present* to Dublin ? Is Protestant Oxford or Protestant Cambridge to be preferred to a University founded by the Holy See, and supported by the whole Irish Church ? You say, and perhaps truly, "that feelings of national prejudice have in fact had no share in keeping English Catholics away from the University of Dublin." What then keeps them away ? Not the want of able Professors ; no, but the want of that social prestige which is thought to be gained by a residence at either of the two great English Universities. This is the only meaning I can put on your words when you say that "English, like Irish, Catholics have for the most part kept away from it, because its claims to be a University, in the true sense of the word, have not yet been sufficiently recognized to inspire general confidence." In other words they keep away from it, because it has not been sufficiently long-established. Well, that is a disease which will mend every day. But for my part I think they keep away from it, because they have a mean hankering after Protestant social recognition and Protestant social rewards ; and because in their hearts they are half-ashamed of what they think the antiquated ways of their spiritual Mother. I have again and again seen this feeling in young men: and I have blushed for their unmanliness, their want of generosity, and their want of courage.

I will now jot down a few remarks on some of your arguments as they come.

1. If the demand for Catholic University Education be so small, (as you say it is,) why not begin with a small University, and let it increase with the increasing wants of our people? There is no reason why an English University could not get on with a few students. Allowing to the full all that you say, you do not seem to me to have answered your own examples of Leyden and Griefswald. And when you say that Universities can exist without being recognized by the state, but not without being recognized by society; what do you mean by society? Do you mean Protestant Society or Catholic Society or both? Do you mean that a Catholic University cannot exist without being recognized by Protestant Society? If so, I cannot of course agree with you. And if a University is not supported at its beginning how is it to obtain that recognition and status of which you speak? Again, you seem to want to do the very same thing with a University which you complain of our wanting to do in the case of young men. You say that they have to swim for their lives but that we wish to keep them on dry land till we teach them how to swim. This is an unfair representation of what we do wish; but it is exactly

what you seem to wish in the case of a Catholic
University. Young men are to keep away from it
till it obtains a recognized social position; it must
remain empty till it is full. Indeed that would be a
very long process. You say: "Time and numbers
are important conditions of this success." Well
then, whilst time is going on, give numbers, now to
the Dublin University; and then to one founded in
England, as soon as it is founded; and both will
succeed. But your argument here seems to be this:
No University will do for us unless it has been established at least many hundreds of years, for without this it has not the necessary prestige. But
Dublin has only been established for a few years;
therefore it will not do. A Catholic University
founded in England will necessarily be in a worse
position than Dublin in this respect; *a fortiori* it
will not do. But a long-established University with
a great prestige will do, whatever its character may
be. Oxford is such a University: *ergo.* And here
I wish to ask you one question. From what you
know of the advocates of this plan, do you think
they would be content with a Catholic University
if it were established; or would they even in that
case prefer a College at Oxford or Cambridge? If
you say it depends on the advantages offered, I ask
you if no sacrifices have to be made for the Faith?
I say this because, firstly, you do not say a word for
Dublin as a temporary provision for English Students;
and secondly, I can see no sign in your Letter that

you would prefer a Catholic University in England, if it could be established, to the proposed College at Oxford; and thirdly, speaking of University Education you say that "any body of men excluded from it will be, as regards Education, and the necessary consequences of Education, in an extremely inferior position to those who have been able to profit by it."

2. You say that the Church cannot provide intellectual culture for her children within herself, because when our Lord gave the Apostles their commission to teach all nations, they do not seem to have understood the commission as having any reference to secular knowledge. Now I will express my opinion of this argument in your own words and then you cannot be offended : " It is hardly possible to conceive anything more silly than this." This is not a convenient tu quoque, but the simple truth. And as you have applied these words to an argument of your adversary, you can not object to their being applied to one of your own. I am justified in saying that you apply these words to the argument of your adversary, for though you might say that you applied them to an argument which he supposes to be used by one of the advocates of the "Oxford scheme," (and a precious scheme it is); yet if that argument be as silly as you say, it surely was silly to put it in. Well now I must say why this argument of yours is so absurd. You say that the Church cannot provide this secular instruction because she has no Divine commission to

do so. Has the state a Divine commission in this matter? Have any secular teachers this Divine commission which you must consider necessary from what you say? If they have it not, how can they teach secular knowledge any more than the Church? At the lowest the members of the Church have as much brains as their neighbours. In what way does a Divine commission to teach supernatural knowledge make those who have it less able to teach secular sciences, than those who have it not? Does supernatural knowledge paralyze all the faculties of the soul and the mind? In what way are St. Augustin, St. Bonaventure, Albert the Great, Scotus, St. Thomas, Suarez, Vasquez, and De Lugo less likely to be right in scientific or philosophical researches than persons who are neither Saints nor theologians? You must by this objection mean one of two things, either that secular teachers have a Divine commission to teach secular knowledge, which the Church has not, or that the commission being necessary and not existing, there can be no possibility of such teaching at all. For you say: "We have never heard that any promise of Divine guidance has been attached to the Church with reference to such knowledge." We also have never heard of any such promise; but neither have we ever heard that it was wanted. You say: "without such a promise it is impossible that the duty of providing the intellectual culture formed upon it could have been fulfilled." Has then "purely human science" had this promise? Has "anti-christian science" had it? If they have not, where is your argument? This last sentence of yours, which I have quoted, taken in another way is a mere truism. If intellectual culture cannot be formed " without a promise," and no promise exists, then I allow, as you say, that the "culture formed upon it" cannot exist. But what do you gain by that? I must say that your argument at this point is incredible confusion.

3. You next have a good deal to say on what you call "the equivocal use of the two terms 'Catholic Church' and 'create'." Verbal criticism is always a miserable thing and in this case it is a dead failure. Every one reading the passage you criticize must see that the word "create" is used, not in its theological sense, but in its popular acceptation. And the whole meaning of the passage is as plain as possible. Oxford was a creation of the Catholic Church in the sense of being moulded, formed, and developed, according to the spirit of the Church at that time. As a bullet takes the form of the mould in which it is cast, so Oxford was shaped in the mould of the Church. I mean this for nothing more than an illustration. Inanimate matter cannot exactly represent the truth about living intelligences. When you say that the Establishment is a creature of the state, as it is, you do not, I suppose, mean that the state made it out of nothing. And yet you might just as well find fault with the word "crea-

ture" in this sentence, as with the word "create" as used in the sentence of which you speak. But surely when you make so much ado about this word you should be very particular yourself. We ought to be careful about throwing stones when we are in glass houses. And yet what do you say? " To create is in reality to make out of nothing. A Catholic University in England would at the present day be a very near approach to a creation ex nihilo." If creating is making out of nothing, what is a creation out of nothing, or " a creation ex nihilo," as you call it? I should never have thought of alluding to this if you had not been so hard on this word 'create.' And I may say that I could here note three passages at least where your words, as they stand, have no meaning, though it is very easy to see what you intend to mean. I may also take this opportunity of saying that I have not spoken about your letter to the writer of the Review : and consequently have no notion what he thinks of these passages on which I am commenting. Nor indeed have I had any, but the very slightest, conversation with him on the subject at all.

4. "The gravest Fathers recommended for christian youth the use of Pagan masters : the most saintly Bishops and authoritative Doctors had been sent by Christian parents to Pagan lecture-halls." Do you mean this to be an argument for sending Catholics to Protestant masters and Protestant lecture-halls? You say " that the language of the

very Christian Fathers who are known to have
been most intolerant of error shows how utterly
foreign to their minds would have been the
principle which the Dublin Reviewer assumes
to be the only possible one for Catholics to admit."
Am I to understand then that you see no difference between attendance at Pagan and at Protestant lecture halls? Do you mean to say that
you think instruction given by Pagans as dangerous
to the faith of those who receive it, as instruction
given by Protestants? I can hardly believe that
you think this. Every one can see that the nearer
the belief of the instructors is to the belief of the
instructed the greater is the danger. In fact the
danger *must* always vary in an inverse ratio to the difference of the beliefs. Where then, in this case also, is your argument? I must again fall back on
your own words, without which I should have had
a difficulty what to say : "It is hardly possible to
conceive anything more silly than this." Besides,
this example is of no use whatever for your argument. You are very careful to state (and rightly)
that you condemn altogether the plan of sending
Catholics to Protestant Colleges. You advocate a
Catholic College in a Protestant University. But
in the first ages Catholics (because there was
scarcely any danger in this case) were sent to the
Pagan schools of Athens and Alexandria. So this,
if it were any argument in this question, would
make for that which you rightly condemn. What

you must produce as an argument (even from your own point of view,) is a Catholic College in a Pagan University. Yet even that according to our views would in reality be no example for this day.

5. You say that we "argue as if we had the choice between keeping young people on the one hand free from all grave peril and exposing them on the other to the most terrible dangers." I have not the pleasure of knowing any one who would argue in a way so absurd. But do you mean that because we cannot keep them from *all* peril that therefore we are to thrust them into many perils from which we can keep them? If I cannot keep a young man from vice, am I therefore to try to undermine his faith? If we think that a man has a chance of being drowned in crossing the Atlantic, are we therefore to throw him over London Bridge into the Thames, before he starts on his voyage? You say again; "you will not allow a Catholic gentleman to be sent to Oxford, where he will be under strict religious discipline and training; but instead of this he will be sent to Woolwich or perhaps directly into the army, or be made clerk of the House of Lords, or get into one of the West End offices, or follow an English minister to Paris, Berlin, or Vienna, every one of which situations may fairly be regarded as more full of peril to his soul than that from which you would exclude him. Will the Reviewer consent to extend the conclusion of the argument involved in his objection to these and other situations

which might be mentioned? Where will he stop
and why?" Now I will say that I am firmly convinced
that these "situations" are not *more* full of peril to
his soul than that from which we would exclude
him. I will say further that I am convinced they
are not nearly *so* full of peril. But let that pass.
I will tell you *where* we stop and *why*. We stop
at necessity, and because we cannot help it. If
by the will of God a man has to work for his living,
he must take the best situation he can get. If he
does not work he cannot live. Yet even thus I
should think that every one who loves God would
willingly make a great sacrifice of worldly advantages that he might be kept out of spiritual dangers.
Still I see that the very persons who are in most
danger would be least likely to make any sacrifice
for this end. But are we to aid and abet them? Let me
give you an illustration of what I am saying. We allow
Catholic servants to take Protestant places, because
otherwise the poor things would oftentimes starve.
But are we in addition to recommend them, for
instance, to go and hear a Protestant Lecture on
some historical subject when we know that their
faith will be represented in an odious or ridiculous
light? And I may say in passing that, whatever
you may say or think, De Maistre is right, and
"history since the Reformation *has* been in conspiracy against the Church." It is in conspiracy
against the Church now. Are we then to send
these persons to hear such a lecture because we can

not help allowing them to go to Protestant places ? Yet this is the force of your argument, if it has any. "Where will he stop and why"? We stop where common sense, and theology, and the stern logic of facts, compel us to stop. That is the *where* and the *why*.

This will apply to what you say afterwards about law and medicine coming into collision with theology; and about attendance on lectures in Trinity College being a necessary condition for admission to the bar in Ireland. When therefore you say of the Reviewer, " I confess that I cannot see how he can logically stop short of absurdities which I had rather not allude to," you say that which is an extreme absurdity itself. But on the other hand, (though I feel sure you do not see it) the logical consequences of your argument are simply immoral. And so in their case the absurdity is a secondary question.

Now one word more on this point. You say, "Can you prevent a youth of twenty or twenty-one from frequenting the society of his father's friends and being fascinated by their follies and *vices ?*" What is this? Can I believe my eyes? If any father of " a youth of twenty or twenty-one" is so lost to all sense of shame as to have " friends" whose " vices" are likely to fascinate his son : if still further he is not ashamed of degrading himself by throwing his son into their company, then all I can say is that he has forgotten the Day of Judgment and is not fit to approach the Sacraments. How can he be, when he is leading his own son into sin?

There is a sentence in the Review which you quote that runs thus; "there is evidence enough of the injurious effects of English Protestant society upon the Catholics who court it and live much in it." Upon this you remark; "To say nothing of its starting from a supposition which I know to be wholly unfounded in fact, it seems to me to be of an eminently unpractical character." This is a mere question of evidence: *I* am certain that the supposition *is* true, and that it is founded altogether on unmistakeable facts. I know it to be true. I have seen it, and see it; and am I to disbelieve what I see? If I stood alone in this opinion I might be diffident about it: but I am fortified by the opinions of others on every side. Besides, all writers on spiritual science agree that intercourse with Protestants, except for the purpose of converting them, is hurtful to the soul. No one can court Protestant society and live much in it, without losing the brightness of his spiritual vision and, in a great measure, the instincts and sympathies of the faith. What then do you mean by saying that this objection is "of an eminently unpractical character?" Is it "unpractical" to look after the soul? If so, I wish that we were all a good deal more unpractical than we are. But what is the point of your argument here? You say that "the observation starts from a mistaken supposition and is eminently unpractical." What is it that you mean by this? The supposition is either false or true: if false, the objection drawn from it has no value; if true, it has the greatest possible value. Any one can understand that. But to say that the supposition is untrue and the inference unpractical and then to argue about the unpractical inference, is a most wonderful confusion of ideas. Surely any one who pats a "respected writer" on the back, and tells him patronizingly to look after "the categories," ought to be a little more careful himself. How shall I characterize this argument of yours? With your permission, (can you refuse it?) I will fall back again on your own words: "It is hardly possible to conceive anything more silly than this." What should I have done if you had not written this sentence, and got it ready for me?

6 You speak of the "exquisite good sense" which does not allow men "to confound the ideal with the real." This is meant to be a slap at the "unpractical" people who object to the worldliness that comes from intercourse with Protestants; and, God knows, from many other sources too. But it misses the mark. These words, "to confound the ideal with the real," sound well but have literally no meaning whatever. No sane man ever did or ever could do such a thing. I will not say that a monomaniac might not do it; but I do not know that even in such a case it would be possible. For

instance, supposing a man to be real, would he "confound the ideal with the real" if he fancied himself a tea-pot? Not unless a tea-pot be the ideal. But if you mean by this that we think it right always to do what is abstractedly best you unintentionally misrepresent us. We have no such absurd plan of action. I beg to assure you that we have heard of such things as Christian prudence and Christian expedience : we have heard of them and we practise them. But we cannot see that to put souls in unnecessary peril, especially for mere worldly advantages, is either expedient or prudent or just. And therefore as we believe that this "Oxford scheme" is contrary to Christian prudence and Christian expedience and also to Christian justice, we oppose it with all our strength. Often "we see that to attempt more is to effect less : that we must accept so much or gain nothing : and so perforce we reconcile ourselves to what we would have far otherwise, if we could." That "a mixed education may in a particular time or place be the least of evils" I will not altogether deny. But this is not the time and Oxford is not the place for such a scheme. Sometimes necessity compels us to "compromises," but *never* to "violations of principle." We may often have to choose certain positions, which abstractedly we do not like, which if left to ourselves, we would not choose; but that is no reason why we should rush into dangers without any necessity for so doing. You say, "The truth is, that the Church of God is not afraid of such positions when they are manifestly providential and can not be avoided." I do not know what you mean by saying that the Church is not afraid of that which is "manifestly providential." How can she be afraid of anything that her Divine Master sends? And that which is " manifestly providential" comes from Him. I will tell you of what the Church is not afraid and of what she is afraid. She is *not* afraid of any power human or diabolical, but she *is* afraid of disobeying God, and being unfaithful to the Incarnate Word Who bought her with His Precious Blood. She is *not* afraid of any position in which she can be placed, but she *is* afraid of betraying her trust. She never confounds "the ideal with the real," for that is simply impossible : but she makes herself " all things to all men, that by any means she may gain some;" and she always does that which is wisest and best and most prudent, justest and most expedient under the circumstances. That is what the Church does.

7. You continue ; " I am probably to blame in not being able to distinguish between the Reviewer's seventh and eighth reasons." Well, there I agree with you. But if as you say yourself you are probably to blame in not distinguishing, why did you not take the trouble to distinguish ? If on the other hand you think you are not to blame, why do you say that you are ? I do not understand men when they talk in this way. We

cannot commit the Church to a false position, because she is only responsible for that which she does herself. And the Church of course cannot commit herself to any false position, for she is divinely guided. But portions of the Church may be committed to false positions in many ways. The seventh reason then says abstractedly that it is better for individuals to lose faith or piety, than for us to "implicate (any portion of) the Church in relations which involve false principles." The eighth says that "the founding of such a hall would be a public and authoritative sanction, and even invitation," to Catholics to send their sons to Protestant Universities. To commit ourselves to false principles and to invite others to do the same are plainly not the same thing. Truly therefore do you say that you are "probably to blame," if you do not see the difference between these two reasons.

There is one point on which I must now dwell for a moment. I will speak of it more fully further on. Alluding, I suppose, to the seventh reason, you say ; "a rigorism, such as the Church has never yet sanctioned and which quietly contemplates ' the risk to a number of individuals,' nay, ' the loss of any number of individuals,' appears to me likely to place the Church in a far more false position than that which it would occupy by following another course."

I think that you will see, on consideration, that

this sentence ought never to have been written; but that having been written it ought to be retracted. Such a charge, as you have made, ought never to be made against any one, much less against a Priest, who by his office is bound to have a great love for souls, and a great sorrow for their loss, unless it can be most certainly proved. You speak of the rigorism which "*quietly contemplates*" the risk to numbers of individuals. A horrible and a terrible thing, if it be true. But what are the facts? There is not the slightest ground for the charge. I turn to the seventh reason, and I read as follows: "*Much as we deplore* that any should be exposed to the occasion of losing either faith or piety, still *even this must be endured*, rather than" compromise the Church, as far as in us lies. Again: it would be "a *sad* but safer alternative" &c. I told you before that the writer of the Review had expressed no opinion to me on these matters. Consequently I do not know what he has felt about such a charge. I know what I should have felt myself, and I think he must have felt it keenly. I would not leave any one under such an imputation as this, if I could clear him from it. There is no need to defend the Reviewer against such a charge, in the face of the Church. But I say this to you by whom the charge has been made. The *quiet contemplation* of the loss of souls is something terrible beyond thought. And I am able to say, from a long acquaintance with the Reviewer, that this is one of the last things which could justly be laid to his charge. And I will say plainly, for it is better to have it out, that such an accusation is offensive and unjust, in the highest degree. I do not myself care about hard names nor about most kinds of judgments: I can stand many things, I may say most things, very easily, but I could not have stood that. It is for the honor of the whole Priesthood that I resent this charge.

Further, as you find fault with this eighth argument, for the reason you give, you must, if your words express your meaning, take an opposite or at least a different view. But on this point, as the question is stated, there is no different view which is not also an opposite one. Therefore I am justified in supposing that you would put the matter thus: 'Much as we deplore that any portion of the Church should be committed to relations which involve false principles, yet even this must be endured rather than that any harm should come to these persons,' who will have their own way. Now mind I do not say that you mean this. I will bring against you no such charge. But I do say that this is the logical consequence of your words: only fortunately men are not *always* logical. I must, however, add that if this is not your meaning, your objection has no meaning. And that I think is near the mark.

8. Lastly; you say: "Defend the outworks if you please as long as they can legitimately be defended, but the citadel which by itself is wholly im-

pregnable will assuredly be lost if too much import.
ance be attached to their preservation. It is only
by means of these that the walls of the citadel can
be scaled." Such a citadel and such outworks
would indeed be a curiosity. If it is only by these
outworks, as you say, that the walls of the citadel
can be scaled, it was surely bad engineering to put the
outworks there at all. Without them the citadel was
safe. And being thus by itself wholly impregnable,
the engineer, who built outworks by which alone it
could be taken, must have been a traitor or a fool.
But I do not believe that such a thing ever existed
as a fortress altogether impregnable except for its
outworks. If a fortress can be taken when it has
good outworks you may be sure it could have been
more easily taken without them. We do not expect
similes to be perfect on every side. Even Homer's
similes are not altogether exact : we know that,
when they are long, they halt in a good many places. But a simile used for an argument ought not
to be nonsense. And this simile of yours is on the
whole the worst that I have ever seen, as far as I
can remember, except that celebrated one of Mr.
Montgomery's,

> " The soul aspiring pants its source to mount,
> As streams meander level with their fount."

Further, no outwork of the Church ever has
been taken or ever can be taken. Be assured of
that. It is just as possible for the citadel of the
Church to fall as for one of her outworks to fall. If

anything falls, by its falling it is proved not to have been an outwork of the Church. I will only add that a denial of the fact that there are Antipodes was never and could be never, in any sense, an outwork of the Church.

Still on one or two points, we are agreed. And I hope you will believe me when I say that I make no question of your motives though I dislike so intensely your scheme. I do not doubt that your object, as mine, is to promote the good of the Church. We differ about the way, that is all. I make no pretence to a monopoly of zeal : I should be foolish if I did. I therefore respect your motive, though I condemn your plan.

1. I agree with you as to your remarks on so-called Rationalism, down to the quotation, Sæpe expugnaverunt &c." I wish we had a better name for that form of misbelief. Catholics are the only persons who reason logically from the Revelation of God, and it is only in and by the Church that the human reason can be perfected. I think that it is at least just as bad to deny the Infallibility of the Church as it is to deny the Inspiration of the Scriptures. And unbelief about the Blessed Sacrament seems to me as pernicious and more illogical than unbelief in the Incarnation. As there is no rational resting-place between denying the possibility of all miracles, and testing each miracle, now or at any other time, on its own evidence, as the Church does; so there is no rational resting-place between sub-

mission to an infallible authority external to our-selves and submission to our interior light, whatever it may be. For submission to an external authority, which is not Divine and infallible, is absurd. And to this day it is a mystery to me how men can be-lieve in God, and yet believe that He, the Eternal Father, has cast His creatures adrift in this world without an infallible authority, to show them the Truth and keep them in it.

Bishop Colenso has reasoned truly, starting from the principles of the Reformation. If the other Bishops and the ministers of the Establishment do not all agree with him, it is because they have not dared to follow out their principles to a logical conclusion; but each one has stopped at some arbitrary point, without rhyme or reason. And in passing, I may say that it would be almost impossible, I think, to find any remarks more inconsistent, inconsequent, and meaningless, than those of the Bishop of Lincoln on Bishop Colenso, which just lately have been printed in the papers. What are we to think of ra-tional men, who refer to external authority in spirit-ual matters, meaning by that, a judgment of law-lords and Bishops, or a fortuitous concurrence of ar-ticles, or any of the many standards and confessions of faith, which men, forsaking the guidance of the Church, have devised from time to time? Indeed I think we may say truly of Bishop Colenso what Macaulay in effect said untruly of the schoolmen: It is wonderful how a man of such natural sagacity, could ever have been satisfied with the miserable premisses from which he starts.

2. More than all I agree with you as to those words, which you have made your own most fully and unreservedly: "that no amount of intellectual culture or social advantage can be weighed in the scale against the least measure of fidelity to the Catholic faith and Catholic morality." Now most sincerely I thank you for asserting this great and vital principle so heartily. I can not but have friendly feelings towards you when you say that. The more that any one attempts to make the name of God heard, in this deafening noise of Babylon, the more my heart turns towards him. I love any man and every man, in the Church and out of the Church, who, according to his light and strength, stands up manfully for God, against the world and the devil.

But this is the very reason why I turn away so strongly from your Letter; for I think that what you say does not tend to advance the cause of God, though you may think that it does. My reason and my feelings, my whole mind and instincts, are against the plan you advocate. I am convinced it is full of deadly perils for souls : but I have no fear and no alarm about it, for I am also convinced that it will never succeed. Though, as I said, I am entirely ignorant about the authorship of this Letter, yet, to say truth, I can not pretend to be ignorant of the source from which it comes. That is clear, or at least I think that it is clear. You must, I imagine be one of the writers in the Rambler, and the Home and Foreign Review. At any rate your Letter smells of that Home and Foreign Review, which now, by the blessing of God and the watchfulness of the Holy See, is like Troy. On that erratic Periodical, happily for the Church in England, the Extinguisher stands for ever. I would say more of it here if it were up and strong; but I do not wish to kick even a book when it is down. If you never had anything to do with that publication and did not approve of the line it took, (for convenience I speak of the two as one), then I hereby apologize to you for thinking so; pleading for excuse what I consider the strong family likeness.

I have now a few remarks to make on this plan in particular and also generally on our position.

1. The opponents of this Oxford scheme feel it to be a question of the most vital importance, but they also feel that the issue does not rest with them. The final appeal must be to that authority, whose decision is law to all Catholics. This being so, it would be absurd to say much of that which they are prepared to do in defence of their view. I will therefore only say that, if it did depend on them, they would feel it to be a question on which they could, so to say, neither give nor take quarter. But still as the question is being discussed it is open to any one to show us that we are wrong if he can. Only on this question and on all questions the trum-

pets on both sides ought not to give an uncertain sound. If any man thinks I am wrong let him prove it and I will acknowledge it at once. All that I stipulate for, is that he shall not begin by saying that he thinks I am nearly right, and then set to work to prove that I am altogether wrong. I trust that we shall always write with proper courtesy one towards another : at the same time I like every man to call a spade, a spade, and say plainly what he thinks. We ought to say what we mean, and mean what we say, for we are in perilous days, and more perilous days are coming, if the signs of the times be true. As long as the dykes are strong and sound we can keep out the flood. But who can tell the effect of one rat-hole ? And if once the waters rush out, then woe to the fruitful plains. Still we are not anxious in this matter, for we are persuaded that the plan can never be carried out. I do not believe that either Oxford or Cambridge will ever agree to it : and even if they were to agree to it, and the Church were to suffer the plan to be tried, I am certain that it would never work. You have settled no doubt in your own mind that the right thing is to put the bell on the neck of the cat, but though I am no prophet, yet I can venture to say that it will be a long waiting before any one hears the tinkling of *that* bell. And indeed if Oxford offered to receive us as proposed, that very fact would in itself be an argument and a strong argument against the plan. I wish that quotation about the Danaos and their dona were not so hackneyed, for it is a good quotation after all: as true now as it was in the days of Virgil. What have we done for them, and what could they gain, that we should at once trust the advances of those who by the necessity of the case must theologically be our enemies? And turning from them to ourselves how many do you expect would be on your side? I believe that the numbers of those who are said to be wishing for this College are counted by tens when they ought to be counted by ones. I feel certain that the estimate of their numbers is greatly exaggerated, and that like fame that estimate " vires acquirit eundo." Poll the Priests of this land and eleven out of twelve will be against you: poll the laity and five out of six will be against you. I have such a respect for our laity as a body that I do not doubt and cannot doubt, but that they would without a pang cast all worldly advantages behind their backs, if they had to be purchased by the least peril to their childrens' souls. And may God bless all who do this. You say; " This great question is at this very moment solving itself whether we will or no." To that I answer, This great question can not solve itself nor can we solve it. It can be solved only by the Holy See. And " those members of our clergy, nobility, and gentry," to quote your own words, "who are directly interested in the question of University Education can not be impressed with too lively a conviction," that all that we can do in this matter is to talk, and that it is for the Holy Father and only for him to act. In many questions the Holy Father consults the wishes and, sometimes even the prejudices of those over whom he rules, when he can do so without injury to them : but this is a question in which he can consult no one except himself and that Divine Master Whose Vicar he is. You say that " the interests both of religion and education will assuredly suffer the most deplorable loss if we persist in shutting our eyes to what is going on around us." But we ourselves, in religion and in education, will assuredly suffer a far more " deplorable loss," if we persist in opening our eyes on the world and its advantages, and in shutting them on God and the Vicars of His Son. What we have to do therefore is to ask the Holy See for its decision in this matter, and cheerfully accept the answer, whether it be for us or against us. · I feel as strongly as any one can against this plan, but if the Holy See decided in its favor I should think that it was wise and good. I do not mean that I would stick to my own opinion and preserve a respectful silence about the Holy Father's decision. That is a course which is simply beyond my comprehension. I have never been good at splitting hairs, and before one could be able to do anything like that, the amount of hair splitting to be got through is something perfectly appalling to contemplate. Sometimes indeed in indifferent matters, "a man, convinced against his will, is of the same opinion still." But there is no room for this process as to

s of the Apostolic See. To keep our own
l preserve a respectful silence when Rome
is intellectually childish and morally ???
th intellectually and morally altogether
the spirit of the Church. It may be ???
at do you say about these matters not
the promise of the infallibility of the
will tell you what I say. By the Divine
Church is immediately and directly in
ll questions of faith and morals. But
he is also infallible on dogmatic facts.
in, as we know from the case of Jansen,
h she can form no supernatural judgment
which do not touch dogma or come into
h it, yet the moment that an infallible
out facts is necessary for defining an ???
or condemning a proposition, then she is
that judgment, for otherwise the Pro-
??? failed. Thus she decided on the fact
Propositions were in the book of Jansen
same way she judges infallibly about
g to morals, as in the Canonization of
I say then further that she is able to
bly about dogmatic *theories* as well as
???. If any system of physics, metaphy-
or psychology, comes into collision with
e can judge infallibly about it. Thus
eley held (or thought he held or did not
e did not hold) a certain theory about
Church directly could form no super-

natural judgment about that. Her natural judgment, the judgment of her metaphysicians and theologians, would indeed cæteris paribus, at the very least, be as good as his; but as yet there would be nothing supernatural. But suppose that this theory clashes with her dogmas about the Blessed Sacrament, then at once she can decide infallibly whether such a doctrine is in his book, "as a dogmatic fact; and whether it be true, as a dogmatic theory." Again, if Sir W. Hamilton holds that the existence of God can not be demonstrated, (I am not speaking of mathematical demonstration,) and if on the other hand the Church has decreed that no man, except through his mortal sin, can be ignorant of God for any length of time, then plainly she must give up her office of a Divine Teacher, or else be able to decide infallibly whether this theory be in his books; and whether it be contrary, in its issues, to the Faith. And that the existence of God can be demonstrated is also the express teaching of Holy Scripture: for St. Paul says: "The invisible things of Him from the creation of the world are clearly seen, being understood by the things that are made; His eternal Power also and Divinity: so that they are inexcusable." But St. Thomas says, "This cannot be, unless the existence of God can be demonstrated from created things; for that which must first be understood about anything is whether it exists or not. Thus from creatures the existence of God can be demonstrated, though, as these creatures are not proportionate to

Him, we can not from them know Him perfectly as
to His Essence." So a system of ethics, which would
make it impossible to hold the vicarious Sacrifice of
our Lord, must come accidentally within the range
of her Infallibility. I say the same of any of the
new systems of psychology, supposing for instance
that one or more of them be found to contradict the
true doctrine about the Hypostatical Union. Consequently whatever the Holy See may decide on this
question must be right. For thus it comes indirect-
ly within the range of her infallible decisions. And
I should receive that decision with full interior as-
sent, even if it should be against me. I should think
that I had, in forming my opinion, overlooked some
important principles or facts which altogether alter
the aspect of the question. That is my view of the
matter.

2. The Church never can be afraid of any discoveries of science, for the same God Who created the
world revealed the Bible, and established His Church.
Therefore it is simply impossible for any discoveries
of geology or astronomy to contradict the Sacred
Scriptures or the Creeds or any of the teaching of
the Church. I can see God in the flowers and the
trees, in the mountains and the sea, in the earth and
the stars, as plainly as I can see Him in Isaias or the
Psalms or the Gospel and Apocalypse of St. John.
He is seen in the creatures of His Hand as He is
seen in the Apostles' Creed, or the Creed of Pope Pius,
or the Dogmas and Definitions of the Church.

Therefore no questions about scientific or other discoveries can disturb any one who has faith. We can sincerely rejoice in all discoveries, if they be true, and in all material progress that is for the well-being of our race. But we must be allowed to suspend our judgments when we see that wonderful discoveries, certain and ascertained facts of to day, become certain and ascertained falsehoods of to-morrow. Science of every kind at this moment is always changing. If you read a book on any physical science, and then forget that science for a while, and after two or three years take up another treatise on the same subject, it is perfectly astonishing to find how many things, once held certain, are given up, and how much is believed that before was doubted. We have been told for instance that the sun is 882,000 miles in diameter and that its mean distance from the earth is 95,000,000 miles. From this, the velocity of light is given at 192,000 miles a second. This has long been thought to be settled. But now the greatest astronomers think that there is some very large error as to the distance of the sun from us. To determine this more accurately they are making great preparations for observing the next transit of Venus over his disc. That transit used to be expected in 1874; but I believe that the year in which it is now settled that it will take place is 1882. If it should turn out that the error in the sun's mean distance from us is as great as is expected, what are we to think of all the calculations that have been based upon that distance?

And astronomy is generally reckoned as one of the surest of the sciences. Of course this question of the distance of our earth from the sun affects all calculations of the specific gravities of the fixed stars and planets, and the general principle of gravitation. I only give this as one instance. The conclusions of science must be more certain than they are before they can influence theology. Has the Church to trouble herself about these ever-changing phases of human opinion? When a thing is absolutely certain it is time for her to give her attention to it. I go on further to say, at the risk of being misrepresented, that the importance of all our material progress is most absurdly exaggerated. And this is intimately connected with what I am saying. There are two things that men are always doing in these days. They exalt the material most foolishly above the intellectual; and still more foolishly they set the intellectual above the moral. Now material progress in civilization and the comforts of mankind is good; but let a due proportion be observed in these things. Take for instance Macaulay's Article on the Baconian philosophy; it is simply pernicious and detestable beyond expression. Most truly did Emerson say of him that in his writings he degraded the human intellect to the rank of a saucepan. Utterly mistaken and wrong as Emerson is we can not but feel much sympathy with him in many points; but as to Macaulay there is scarcely a single point on which we can have any sympathy with him at all. He is the

Coryphæus of the saucepan philosophy. I will say the truth; I value very lightly many of our material triumphs, and much of our boasted progress. The end for which we are sent into this world is God, And I do not see that these things make men better or in any way unite them more to Him. Railways and electric telegraphs are all very well in their way; as a matter of convenience it is better to have them than to be without them, but what do they do for the salvation of souls, or for the glory of God? Men answer and say, O, but all these discoveries and inventions bring more knowledge of the works of God. I acknowledge that; but I ask, Do they bring with them more knowledge of God Himself? Do they bring with them more love of God? For that is the point. I do not see that these modern discoveries do anything for the preaching of the Gospel. That message of glad tidings cannot be preached by electric telegraph. Business of the world may be helped by this; but not our Father's business. Again, as to railways; if we can go quicker over the earth to make God known, so also can the teachers of error go along with us to obscure Him. If the Church on an emergency can send a message more quickly than of old, her enemies can do the same. If the truth can be scattered more widely by means of the printing press, so also falsehoods are more widely spread. The fact is that the relative positions of the servants of God and the servants of the world are much what they always were. These discoveries

of which we boast so much are made in the lowest
scale of creation, for inanimate matter is lower by
far than the beasts of the field and the birds and
fishes and reptiles. I am glad that all these discoveries should be made, because God created inanimate
matter and it represents some idea in His Divine
Mind; and He has given us our intellects which we
may exercise on it. But let these things keep
their place and not seek to intrude into an order to
which they have no right of entrance. Then I can
regard them with pleasure and even with a certain
degree of reverence. It was in days on which we, in
our pride of intellectual and material progress, look
down with pity, that St. Francis Xavier and Blessed
Peter Claver went forth, to the East and West, in
the strength of the Son of God, and stormed the very
strongholds of Satan. It was then that the voices of
those mighty Apostles rang, like clarions, through
the world, proclaiming the tidings of Redemption to
those who were sitting in darkness and the valley of
the shadow of death. Where is there now in these
enlightened days a man stirring the great heart of
Christendom, dragging men from the world and lift-
ing them up to God, as St. Francis did, by his burning
words of love? Where is there a man strong and
majestic, like my own St. Charles, moulding and
fashioning mens' hearts by the pattern of the Gospel,
building up whatever may be broken down, and thril-
ling the whole Church by the fire of his own burning
heart? What are our material triumphs to triumphs

like these? What is knowledge without love? If by the knowledge of new chemical affinities and the discovery of new stars, a man feels himself lifted to God and more filled with love for Him, then, I say, work at chemistry and astronomy night and day. But if the sun should be found to be 150 millions of miles away, shall I love God either less or more than I do now, when its distance is supposed to be 95 millions? Vega is said to be 75 millions of millions of miles away; what difference will a few millions of miles make? It is contrary to reason to believe that in such a distance there can be even an approximation to truth. Now do not say that I see no good in astronomy and other physical sciences. That would not be the truth. But I say again let them keep their own place, and do their own work. And do not let them and their uncertainties be set up against that teaching of the Church, whatever it may be, which is just as certain and true as God. But if these things bring no spiritual benefit, what is the use of them? Again I shall have the answer, To teach us more about God and His Works. And again I say what is the good of that, unless it unites us more to Him? And indeed all these discoveries are merely questions of degree. The knowledge that we have of God in the greatest and most wonderful of His Works (I am speaking of His works in the order of nature) is the same in kind that we have by looking at a daisy. Abraham and Job saw the glories of this world and the beauty of the sun, moon, and stars as we see them; and the discovery of Uranus or Neptune or Terpsichore does not sensibly in my mind increase my wonder or my love. Suppose it could be settled whether the corpuscular or the undulatory theory of light be true, what advantage would it be? If a man believes in the corpuscular theory, how is he worse? Or if another believes in the undulatory theory, how is he better? Or suppose that both theories be wrong, what does it matter? It will not make us love God less or more. I love and reverence God in all His Works; and so I cannot of course find fault with men for investigating these works, so glorious and so wonderful. I complain of them seeking knowledge *for its own sake*, and forgetting that there is a due proportion even in the works of God. Thus as I said, they set the material above the intellectual and the intellectual above the moral. If Herschel used to sit up night after night to watch the stars, he is a martyr to science, and his zeal in the pursuit of knowledge can never be sufficiently praised. But if a Saint stays up night after night on his knees to hold communion with the Creator of the stars, with Jesus, Himself the Morning Star of a far more glorious world, he is at once set down as a fanatic or an enthusiast. Scientific men who make discoveries in the natural world are to be commended; but they who make discoveries in the spiritual world, that is, the Saints and the theologians of the Church, and indeed all humble, childlike souls who walk with God, are to be condemned, or passed by with a contemptuous sneer. And this is the spirit of the age. This is the spirit of those to whom some persons wish our youth to go for their education. But it is not the spirit of truth. On the contrary it is the spirit of falsehood. All the gifts of nature are as nothing compared with the smallest gift of grace. All this material creation, wonderful, glorious, majestic, as it is; all planetary systems, stretching away into the depths of space; all possible creations that ever may be, are as nothing in the sight of God compared with one victory of one soul over one temptation. And yet men do not see this and will not see it. They multiply books of useful or useless knowledge, compendiums of every science under the sun, encyclopædias, and I know not what: and these things shut God out instead of bringing Him into sight. They keep on making discoveries of wonderful mysteries, but these things are not referred to Him by Whose laws those mysteries exist.

There are people who think that some discoveries in the natural order are dangerous because they contradict or seem to contradict a revealed truth. But this is an idle fear. We need never disturb ourselves for one moment about the Revelation of God. Wisdom is justified in her works of the natural order as well as in her children. If any supposed discoveries of science do really contradict Revelation they are necessarily untrue. And if they need to be harmonised with Scripture or the teaching of the Church, it must be shown that this can be done if they are to be believed. If they can not be so harmonized, the worse for them. God is true and the Church is true and the Bible is true. All science, all metaphysics, all philosophy of every kind, must be brought into harmony with the Faith, not the Faith with them.

Now (to show that intellectual knowledge does not necessarily lead to the truth) Newton was a great man intellectually, and yet he was supremely ignorant of Divine Truth. When he brought that intellect which was so soaring in the physical world to the study of Revelation, most lamentable was the failure. The strong man became weak and the piercing eye was smitten with blindness. He was an Arian, actually ignorant of His Creator, and that sublime Mystery of the Ever-Blessed Trinity, which is known to every little Catholic child. What a degradation: as far as his eternal state was concerned he had far better have been unable to read or write and yet have known his catechism; had far better have carried a hod and frequented the Sacraments. The *Principia*, in the natural order, is a great work, but what is the *Principia* to *The Imitation of Christ*? *The Imitation*, I am certain, has taken thousands of souls to Heaven. Did the *Principia* ever help one man to overcome a temptation and keep from sin? A person will say, That is not the end for which it was written, judge it in its own order and it is good. He says the truth, and I agree with him fully. I only insist upon this that we are not to set a disproportionate value upon these things and by so doing be led to seek for them in an inordinate way. Food is good for the body, and food is good for the soul; each in its own order. Oftentimes in every day we ask God to bless the food which He gives us, and again we thank Him for it. But would it not be the height of folly to compare that food for the body with the precious Food that is provided for the soul? And yet this is exactly what people do, who exalt the natural world out of its proper place. As God is above creatures, as Heaven is above earth, so the spiritual world is above the natural world; and the life of the soul above the life of the body. I feel how easy it is for any one to misrepresent what I have been saying, but I feel also that I have been dwelling on a truth most necessary in these days of materialism; and therefore I have said it. And all that I have been saying is part of a whole and bears upon this subject taken as a whole.

3. I come to the question of worldliness. This is a subject far too deep and important for me to enter upon now. I merely want to look at one or two phases of this spirit, which bear upon the subject in question.

First, I observe that it is the fashion with a certain class of Catholics (fortunately they are very few in number) to disparage every thing Catholics do in literature or science or art. We are such a miserable set of know-nothings that it is a great condescension on their part to have anything to do with us. But

they are kindly disposed towards us, and are willing
to teach us if we are are willing to be taught. If
we will only give up our old light (which I may say
on the whole has served us about as well as we
could have expected) they will turn on us a new
light of the most unheard-of brilliance. They think
it is the sign of a great mind to fraternize with Protestants as far as they can. They are always la-
menting the degraded state of our literature. We can
not spell or say our multiplication tables; and of such
a thing as history we have never heard. We either
hold views which are contrary to history, or if they
wish to talk grandly they say that we hold them
in such a way that they are contrary to the philosophy of history. I can not exactly say what this
may mean. Perhaps a view according to the philosophy of history may be something like this: you
would believe that all the German Electors about
the time of the Reformation were models of every
virtue, and that the Popes about the same time
were just the reverse. Or again, going higher, at
any rate we know nothing of Conic Sections or the
Integral Calculus or Indeterminate Equations: we
are ignorant of Fluxions or Crystallography or Hy-
drodynamics. Then perhaps they say, What a state
education is in amongst us; we doubt if you could
find a single boy at Oscott or Ushaw or Stonyhurst
who could write a decent copy of Iambics or Alca-
ics. But amongst Protestants they find wise and
learned men and clever boys who know these things

and who can do them, and having set up their image they fall down and worship.

There is a view of religion prevailing amongst a few men of strong digestions and great physical powers, which is called muscular Christianity. This is the lowest and meanest view of Christianity which has ever been devised by the misguided intellect of man. Such a view cannot exist in the Church, because it is not possible that any one can hold it who has any knowledge whatever of Divine grace, whether that knowledge be theoretical or practical. But there is something quite analogous to it to be found in the Church; and that is the worship of intellect for itself, and a mistaken view of the part which that power performs in the growth of the soul in grace. And yet nothing can be more absurd than this. We might just as well worship strength of body as strength of intellect. God gives us both. And I love Him for all the bodily health and strength which He gives to His creatures, as I love Him for all the intellectual strength which He gives them: but I am not going to forget the Giver in the gifts, or think that either of them have any value except as they lead to Him. Yet all this complimentary attitude of mind towards the scholarship and science of Protestants to the disparagement of that which is to be found in the Church, is the worship of mere strength of mind. Satan had a most marvellous intelligence, but he did not manage to make good use of it. Who would not rather be

an idiot than use intellect as he used it? All who
worship the intellect apart from Divine grace and
the love of God are in similar danger. And there
are many men who do so, I call this intellectual
worldliness. Such men are ashamed of their breth-
ren and desire the learning of Egypt. Moses was
learned in all the learning of the Egyptians; but
I never heard that he was anxious to send the
Israelites back to Heliopolis to finish their education.
Learning is good if it be used for God, but unsanctified
learning can not lead to Him. I can hardly trust myself to speak of these men. Is it nothing to them that
the Church of God for 300 years in this land has
been in garrets and cellars? Is it nothing to them
that our Priests were proscribed, hunted like dogs,
and hanged? That our laymen were persecuted and
despoiled of their possessions for their fidelity to the
old Church and the old Faith? Have the sufferings
of these Martyrs and Confessors to be forgotten?
If our education is not what it ought to be, what one
day it will be; if our Churches are not what they
ought to be, and one day will be also, why do these
men not pour out the vials of their anger on those
who robbed us of our Universities and Cathedrals
and Parish Churches, and sent us adrift into the
world to provide for ourselves as best we might?
Why do they not keep a little of their carping and
querulousness and complaining for them? Why
has it all to be kept for us? And why do they not
put their shoulders to the wheel and help forward

the cause of education amongst us, instead of preaching to us about our ignorance and assuring us that science and learning are only to be found amongst Protestants? Can any one point out to me a tone of mind more ungraceful, peevish, and petulant, more fretful and unfilial than this?

Next, I observe that many Catholics are most anxious to stand well with Protestants and be well received in Protestant society. They have a great desire that Protestants may think them presentable and so on, and they act accordingly. They are dazzled by the glare of polished Protestant society and they will be satisfied with the fruit from no other tree. They think that, by adapting themselves to the tone of those amongst whom they mix, they will show how refined some Catholics can be and so raise all Catholics in the estimation of their Protestant fellow-subjects and possibly draw some of these selfsame Protestants towards the Church. Could there be any greater ignorance of God and the ways of God? When Israel passed through the Red Sea, Moses, the servant of God, did not hold a reed of Egpyt over the parted waters. It is not by being in the height of the fashion that deliverance for the captives can be wrought. Yet there are many who seem to think so. And I call this moral worldliness.

Let me dwell for one moment on one manifestation of this spirit of worldliness. I mean the marriage of Catholics with Protestants. It is beyond my power to see how any Catholic with a true love for God and the Sacred Heart can marry a Protestant. For a Protestant disbelieves much of that which such a person cherishes, or ought to cherish most. In one sense he disbelieves it all by denying the Infallibility of the Holy See and believing what he does believe on a wrong principle. He also has no well-grounded and well-informed love for those in Heaven whom such a Catholic loves or ought to love. I do not say that such Catholics have not a love for God (for the mind of man is so inconsistent and so forgetful of consequences that it is impossible to say what may be, or what may not be) but I say that I can not see how they have it. When they do such a thing they do not absolutely commit a sin, for the Church can not give permission to any one to commit sin. Still we must remember that she gives her permission for marriage with Protestants very reluctantly and because of the hardness of mens' hearts. But though such an action is not a sin, it is inexpressibly mean. What right have I to say this? I will tell you. There are these words in the Bull of a Pope: "a mixtis matrimoniis abhorret Ecclesia," the Church turns away with abhorrence from mixed marriages. I wish these words were written in letters of gold and put up in every Catholic home. As in this case the Church does not turn away from sin, from what does she turn away? She does not turn away with abhorrence from nothing. I think it is from that which is mean and ungenerous and worldly, and in that sense dishonoring to the Heart of her Lord.

Let me here set down some words of that immortal Pope, Benedict the XIV., one of the greatest and grandest of the Apostolic line. They are in the Bull "Matrimonia," Nov. 4th, 1741. He says, "dolens imprimis quam maxime Sanctitas sua eos esse inter Catholicos qui insano amore turpiter dementati, ab hisce detestabilibus connubiis, quæ S. Mater Ecclesia perpetuo damnavit atque interdixit, ex animo non abhorreant et prorsus sibi abstinendum non ducant," i. e. "The Holy Father grieves in the first place, as much as he can, that persons are to be found amongst Catholics, who, being shamefully maddened by an insane love, do not from their hearts abhor these detestable marriages which our holy Mother the Church has always condemned and forbidden." He says further; "laudansque magnopere etiam illorum antistitum qui, severioribus propositis spiritualibus pœnis, Catholicos coercere student hoc sacrilego hoc vinculo sese hereticis conjungant; episcopos omnes, vicarios apostolicos, parochos, missionarios et alios quoscumque Dei et Ecclesiæ fidelles ministros in eis partibus degentes, serio graviterque hortatur et monet ut Catholicos utriusque sexus ab hujusmodi nuptiis in propriarum animarum perniciens ineundis, quantum possint absterreant :" i. e. "He praises greatly the zeal of those Bishops, who by threatening severe spiritual punishments strive to keep Catholics from uniting themselves to heretics in this sacrilegious bond. Further, he solemnly and earnestly exhorts and advises all Bishops, Vicars Apostolic, Parish Priests, Missionaries, and all other faithful ministers of God and the Church, to keep all Catholics of both sexes, as far as they possibly can, from contracting marriages of this kind, to the danger of their own souls." I wish however here to say one word. In days gone by persons have contracted these marriages without knowing how much they were condemned by the Church. Indeed I mean to say nothing hard or unkind of such persons. I intend my words for those who in these days act against light. What I say is meant as a warning for the future, not as a reproach for the past.

As therefore all Priests who try as much as they can to stop such marriages are greatly commended by the Vicar of Christ, so on the other hand all who do not do so are virtually reproved. If we do not point out to persons, who wish to contract these marriages, the judgment of the Holy Father about them, *we* are to blame. If we point it out, and they choose to act against it, the fault will not be ours but theirs.

But here I must say what spirit we ought to cultivate in our intercourse with Protestants and Catholics as well: and that is a spirit of mutual respect and forbearance. I speak of this because there are some persons who seem to think that refinement means the worship of fashion, especially Protestant fashion. If we reverence Christ in ourselves and others who have been made His, by Baptism; if we reverence the Hand of God in ourselves and others, whoever they may be, we shall never go wrong in this matter. True refinement is a sense of the Presence of God. The man who stands, so to say, with his head bare before the Eternal King, will always be respectful with true Christian politeness to others whether they be rich or poor. He is no respecter of persons; to him there is no difference between one person and another, except that difference of constituted authority which God has ordained, and which is to be reverenced in the Law and its ministers. This spirit will ensure Christian courtesy and Christian politeness to every one. No one can be inconsiderate of the feelings of others if he reverences Christ in them; nor can he be insincere if he reverences Christ in himself. It gives a man what I may call a chivalrous spirit, makes him courageous and tender and refined, and so saves him from meanness and insincerity and vulgarity and worldliness. I have never seen a vulgar person amongst the poor. Ignorant, rough, and unrefined they may be, but not vulgar. They do not live by those requirements of fashion and maxims of the world, which make men vulgar, by making them insincere in their actions and their words. And as we can not try too much to grow in Christian courtesy and kindness and respect for all, so we can not try too earnestly to keep clear of the world, and all that it has and all that it is. This you will see bears on what I am insisting on, that gifts and blessings of nature are at an immense and almost immeasurable distance beneath the blessings of grace; and that all worldly and social advantages are to be scorned, if they bring with them the least peril for souls. You will agree with me in all this.

I now come to a point at which I may conveniently speak of the charge of rigorism which you bring against the Reviewer. You spoke of it as a rigorism which quietly contemplates the risk to souls, nay the loss of souls, but I merely touched upon it. Now, this charge of rigorism is a very grave charge and not lightly to be made. It is not a charge to be bandied about, in an anonymous pamphlet, against any Priest, still less against a Priest of the age and character and standing of the Reviewer. If a layman has any charge to make against a Priest he can go to the Bishop who is always ready to hear what any of his flock have to say, and if he has a charge against the Bishop he can go to the Holy Father, which is in effect to go to our Lord. But it is not befitting the gravity of this charge or the office and position of the accused to make it, as it has been made in an off-hand way, in a pamphlet without a name. As I said before, since it has been made it ought to be retracted or proved, I consider that you owe an apology to the Reviewer; for even if you could prove this charge (of course you can not) I think you would still owe him an apology for the way in which you have made it. But do you understand what this charge of rigorism is? I must tell you for you do not seem to know that rigorism in dealing with men, when they have sinned, is one thing, but rigorism in keeping them from the occasions of sin is another. You acknowledge that this proposed College at Oxford would be an occasion of sin, otherwise you could not speak as you do of those many safeguards which you consider under the circumstances would be necessary for the young men. Our Divine Master has taught us to say "Lead us not into temptation." We consider that this College would be a terrible temptation and occasion of sin. I wish therefore to ask you what right you have to charge with rigorism any one who opposes the scheme? The rigorism of which theologians speak has to do with the Sacrament of Penance; and *there* no one will ever be a rigorist (in the bad sense) who loves our Lord and the souls for whom He died. But that Holy Sacrament is not now and never has been in question with regard to this matter. In another sense and a good sense all the Saints may be called rigorists from the asceticism of their own lives and the care with which they kept men from sin. But this is not the common meaning of the word and it ought to be kept for that which is commonly meant by it. Having guarded my meaning in this way I go on to say that every one who tries to serve God faithfully will be called a rigorist by the world. St. Charles was called a rigorist and hated accordingly. I desire no better inheritance for my friends and myself than to follow in his steps. I go up higher than St. Charles, to our Lord. He "came eating and drinking" "with publicans and sinners;". His Divine compassion for sinners and His Divine forbearance with them are simply unmeasurable and inexhaustible, yet He said of the occasions of sin, " If thy right eye scandalize thee, pluck it out and cast it from thee." "If thy right hand scandalize thee, cut it off and cast it from thee." "It is better for thee with one eye to enter into life than having two eyes to be cast into hell fire." These are Divine Words. And our Lord said also, against the world, " If any man will come after Me, let him deny himself and take up his cross and follow Me." And remember; we have not only to deny ourselves and make sacrifices for our Lord and our Faith, bodily, but also intellectually and socially. But rigorism is often a name which the world gives to the faithful application of these words; and often they are called rigorists, who, when the truth is told, faithfully preach Christ, His Gospel, and His Cross. The day of His Coming will be a day of honor and blessedness and glory to all who are numbered amongst these.

One word now on a subject springing from all this. The deepest speculations about the natural order in any of its manifestations are the veriest shallows compared to the least thought about God. Take Adam Smith on Political Economy, or Dugald Stewart on the Philosophy of the Human Mind, or Jeremy

Bentham on the Theory of Government and Law; their speculations are considered very profound, yet I say that what are considered deep and wonderful speculations on these subjects are literally, like little pools compared with the simple statement that God is absolutely One in His Essence, and absolutely Three in His Divine Persons. The subjective exercise of the intellect is of course greater in these speculations of which I speak, but that is not the question here. Government and political economy pass away and their place knows them no more, but God remains, the One Eternal, the One Uncreated Present. Wonderful, deep, wide-spread, are the consequences which flow from this great truth. I wish we all thought more of it than we do. There is a philosophy which is sharp and shallow, and there is a philosophy which is wide and deep: and it is a sad thing for any one heedlessly to choose that which is false and leave that which is true.

I am now getting near the end of what I have to say at present. You sum up your Letter by saying that the opponents of this scheme must necessarily condemn the Primitive Church, the Mediæval Church, and the Church of all ages. You may be "firmly convinced" of this, but I am "firmly convinced" of the contrary. For, firstly, your instances and examples taken from the Early Church and her use of Pagan schools have no bearing whatever on this plan of a College in Oxford: but if they be any argument at all (which I have denied), they would be in favor "of the principle of sending Catholic students to Protestant Colleges or Halls ;" of which principle you say yourself "that no one *at present* thinks of defending" it. Consequently in this case you are the person who condemns the Church of the early ages, if your argument has any value. But I should like to know what you mean by the words "at present," which I have put in Italics. Do you mean that a time may probably come when some persons will be ready to defend even that plan, which now on all sides is condemned? It is conceivable that some persons may come to speak to us in this way : 'we are ready to condemn with you the plan of sending Catholics to Protestant Colleges if you will concede to us that for which we are contending, viz., a Catholic College in a Protestant University. If you will not meet us half-way we shall be driven by "peculiar circumstances," to take up new ground, and possibly by those "peculiar circumstances" may be led to see that that is defensible which *at present* we hold to be indefensible.' Is this your meaning? If not, what *do* you mean by these words "*at present*"? If they are not a sort of a threat what are they ?

Secondly, you say that we condemn the Mediæval Church : for the Mediæval Church sanctioned Universities, like Oxford or Cambridge, where "moral and intellectual perils" existed. If your argument has to be good for anything, you must show that the Church not only sanctioned the Universities, but also sanctioned the immoralities and heresies which doubtless did arise amongst such numbers as were gathered together in those seats of learning. Oxford and Cambridge were then Catholic, but though Catholic (and indeed the more for that very reason) the devil took good care to be in the midst of them : though the Church certainly did not sanction his presence.   The Church knows that the tares must grow amongst the wheat till the harvest : and she does the best that she can in an evil world.   But it seems to me perfectly childish to say that because she could not in her own Universities keep her young men from sin, that therefore we are to send them to Protestant Universities where the dangers are a thousandfold greater.   It seems to me also most absurd to say that those who oppose this course condemn the Mediæval Church.   Who is it that forgets "the importance of the categories" here ?   If the Church had sanctioned the immoralities mentioned, I grant you might have something to say ; not otherwise. Besides, let me come to your quotation.   Antony a Wood speaks of " a company of varlets who *pretended* to be scholars."   These are the men whose enormities he describes.   You admit yourself that the number may be grossly exaggerated : but I do not think it matters whether it is or not.   You then say that " Hallam is certainly wrong in making a real distinction between 'varlets' and 'scholars'."   In this case you will not I trust consider me as wanting in due courtesy to yourself, if I choose to follow the opinion of that great historian and impartial writer. But as I said the whole of your case as to this has no bearing on our question.

Thirdly; you say we condemn "the Church of all ages." Well that is a sweeping assertion, and down we must go into the abyss, if it be true. But before I can judge of its truth I must ascertain its meaning, if it has any. By our opposition to this plan we are said to condemn the Early Church which sanctioned the use of Heathen learning, and the Mediæval Church, for no reason whatever, as far as I can make out. All that has been brought forward is that she was unable to keep all students from mortal sin. We knew that before. Neither could she keep all intellectual dangers away. We also knew that before. Are there no moral and intellectual dangers now? When we acknowledge them, do we condemn the Church? But further we are said to condemn the "Church of all ages." For what? "For its toleration of an intercourse between believers and the world which in numberless cases cannot fail to be extremely pernicious." I am perfectly amazed at this sentence. You might, as far as your argument is concerned, just as well have said that London is on the Thames. What has this intercourse between believers and the world to do with the question in hand? No one could have written this sentence, bearing in mind the words of St. Paul where he says that it is impossible for us altogether to avoid keeping company "with the fornicators of this world, or with the covetous, or the extortioners, or the servers of idols; *otherwise you must needs go out of this world.*" What can be plainer than this? But where is there any authority here for exposing young persons to unnecessary dangers, either as to faith or morals? Again, you ought to remember those "categories" of which you reminded the "respected writer"; for your argument seems to me to be this: 'You must live amongst sinners; and therefore you ought to send young men to Protestant Universities. But the Church allows you to live amongst sinners, and has always done so; therefore those who oppose this "Oxford scheme" condemn the Church of all ages.' I say, truly, that this seems to me to be a fair representation of your meaning. And therefore I cannot say that I think your argument conclusive. At least if it be so, it is conclusive only against yourself.

Lastly: you address us thus: "Say at once that Universities, properly so called, are distasteful to you, and incompatible with your views of Catholicism." We do not intend to say anything of the sort. We would say it at once if we thought it, without any invitation to do so; but as we do not think it, we do not intend to say it. But we say at once that Universities *as approved by you* are utterly distasteful to us and incompatible with our views of Catholicism. For you seem to think that the very idea of a University, *properly so called*, involves the necessity of intellectual and moral evils: you seem (and I put

it to every one who has read your Letter to judge between us, and in this case I refer, especially, to your
notes,) you seem, I say, to think that a University
can not in reality be a University without a lit...
... part of a University. And a University...

You proceed: "Explain to us if you can why the
Catholic Church and its Sovereign Pontiffs have always had views on this subject more tolerant than
your own?" I cannot explain what has never been,
nor will be. I deny utterly that the Sovereign Pontiffs have been more tolerant on this matter than
am certain that the Holy Father is not one-sided
in this question, for otherwise he would not have
condemned the Queen's Colleges in Ireland, as he
did. He warned Catholics against sending young men
to them. What is the essential difference between
the Queen's Colleges and this "Oxford scheme?"
Therefore I say to you; Explain to us if you can
why you are arguing for that which is virtually condemned by the Holy Father; the condemnation of
the Queen's Colleges...

You then further say: "Do not advocate the
cause of Universities, if by the term you understand
something quite different from what history recognizes under the name." What history recognizes
under the name I am not prepared to say, nor is it
worth while to enquire. Nor am I prepared to say
what the philosophy of history may teach us
about this. But I know what common sense under-
stands by the name. And as we are in England and

not in Germany; let us steer clear of nebulous lumin-
aries and metaphysical haze. A University is a
University, just as an egg is an egg. Looseness in
faith and morals is neither an essential nor an integral part of a University. And a University can
exist without teaching Protestant metaphysics. But
you seem to me to have got somehow an idea into
your head that there is something in the eternal nature of things which makes it impossible that there
can be more than two Universities in England; and
makes it also impossible that those Universities can
be other than Oxford or Cambridge. Though you
would not say this in so many words yet you argue
as if it were so. Therefore I must again with a
slight change address you in your own words: Do
not advocate for Catholics the cause of Universities,
if by a University you understand *only* a *Protestant*
University, or something quite different from that
which Catholics using their common sense see instinctively to be necessary for themselves.

To make an end; let me now see how we stand.
I come to the following conclusions;

1. Those persons, whoever and whatever they
may be, who send their sons to Protestant Universities, put the souls of their children in grievous peril,
disregard the expressed wishes of the Holy Father,
and cause a very grave scandal to the Church.

2. This scheme for a Catholic College in a Protestant University is simply absurd to say the least; for
a moment's consideration will show any one that the

I

practical difficulties to be overcome are so great that, as I said before, it would never work. But it is something much worse than absurd, for it flies right in the face of the Holy Father's decision with regard to the Queen's Colleges in Ireland.

I understand you to say that the want of this University Education is so great that it must be met: but that the number seeking it is so small that it is impossible to found a Catholic University. Even that small number I believe to be much exaggerated, if we are speaking of Protestant Universities. For what I think myself is this; that there are perhaps very many who are desirous of a University Education for their sons, but *very few*, thank God, who would venture to seek for this in Protestant Universities. A true-hearted Englishman, when he is raised by divine grace to the supernatural order, is instinctively loyal in every thought to the Holy See.

3. The arguments used in its favor make against it instead of for it. I never saw all the evil of the scheme so clearly, nor felt such a strong aversion to it, as I did after reading your Letter. I do not say this for the sake of making a point; it is the truth, and nothing but the truth. I only hope that all persons inclined to favor your scheme may read your Letter. I have no doubt as to the result.

4. Let us get a Catholic University in England. We can easily get it if we please. Will any one try to persuade us that this plan can not be carried through with the help of our laity who are growing

every day in numbers and wealth and influence? Let me give you an instance of what has been done by persons out of the Church? About 20 years ago the Free Church separated from the Established Church of Scotland. It numbered then 700,000 souls; it is now estimated at about 1,000,000. In these 20 years it has built Churches and Ministers' houses in every parish in the land, with perhaps one or two exceptions. It has raised a Sustentation Fund, which pays £200 a year or £150 to every minister who has a Church. It has raised a flourishing University of its own, and would not touch with the tip of its finger the University of the Communion from which it separated. And last year it raised for charitable purposes £343,134. 8s. 9½d. The Church Building Fund alone, for that year, came to £49,314. 7s. 4¼d. These men have not the light of the faith. Will any one try to persuade me that Catholics can not found a University if they please? *We need nothing but a vigorous development of our own resources.* Where there is a will, there is a way.

5. Till this University can be started, any one who wants a University Education can go to Dublin. A University sanctioned and encouraged by the Holy See has some little claim upon Catholics of every nation. And if those who desire this education do not choose to go there, it is ten thousand times better for them to go without such an education altogether, at the risk of any social loss, rather than seek for it amongst Protestants.

1. 6. But if you will only be content with a University which shall be 500 years old on the day of its opening, say so. If no Universities but Oxford and Cambridge will do for you, say so. If you think that there is so little public spirit in our laymen and so little zeal for the glory of God and the good of the Church, that they will not come forward to carry through this plan, say so. If you mean that the Catholic world cannot provide suitable professors, say so. If you would disparage this College at Oxford for spiritual or moral advantages, say why you want it. It is quite useless to say that it is for education which cannot be got elsewhere, for every one knows that education no less good can be got elsewhere. I am sure that those persons who will not go to Dublin will we can go to a University in England are seeking for something else than education. And there complaints about the hardness of their position and the social advantages they lose are rubbish. That is what I think. If again you mean that we ignorant Catholics are such a set of fools that we must go for instruction to Protestants, say so, and point out to us the reasons for this opinion. Also, if you please, indicate to us the places amongst ourselves where the new lights are to be found. And further, explain to us, if you can, why you advocate a scheme which must be distasteful to all our Bishops, because it is contrary to the spirit and traditions of the Holy See, and
7. I know well that new ideas new lights

talk of us who are content with the old way, and I will just note here what it is. They say; "These rigorists mean well but they are utterly unpractical. They live in a world of their own devising and not in this active, bustling, every-day, working world in which we are. They might do very well in Arcadia or Utopia, but they are out of place in England of the nineteenth century. They are always forgetting "the categories," and they are sadly deficient in all that appertains to "the philosophy of history." They have no research, and they are afraid of telling the truth even about the few historical facts with which they happen to be acquainted. Besides this they are always trying to screw people up to the counsels; and they have a most exaggerated idea of the malignity of venial sin, and worldliness. In fact they are not men of the world at all; and though doubtless they are sent into the world for some purpose, it. is difficult to see what that purpose is." Having stated the opinion which some persons hold about us, I think that perhaps the best thing that I can do is to leave it as it stands.

And now I will soon finish what I have to say. For myself I will say that I detest all new ways and all new lights. I love the old way along which so many millions have gone to their rest : and the old light which has shone ceaselessly and brightly through the darkness of so many thousand midnights and the spray of so many thousand storms. I love and trust the Holy See, not only as to faith and morals, but in all its traditions and judgments and ways. Even in natural things, out of its own immediate order, I love its very shadow and trust to it for safety. It is the representative of God in the world; the great barrier against lawlessness of every kind. Both in thought and in action it sets the bounds beyond which no man has a right to go. Freedom of thought is simply a delusion of the devil. A man has no more right to *think* about anything, in any way, he pleases, than he has to *do* anything, in any way, he pleases. If men were allowed to do what they like all governments must perish : and if men were to be allowed to think what they like the spiritual Kingdom would be destroyed. That spiritual Kingdom *is* destroyed, wherever men think as they please. There are men who cut themselves off from the Church and proclaim the right of free enquiry : but they are in a state of intellectual anarchy. It is indeed spiritual anarchy, but that is worse than the other. Thus Protestantism in the logical consequences of its doctrines is antinomian in thought and deed. If every man has a right to enquire for himself, who has a right to blame the conclusions, whatever they may be, to which he sincerely comes ? But the Church sets a guard over her childrens' souls, for she knows what it cost to redeem them : she bears always in mind the Passion and Death of Jesus, His Cross and Precious Blood and Sacred Heart. I always think that nothing shows her divine care and watchfulness more

than the *Index Expurgatorius*. Divinely watchful
for souls she examines the literature of the world,
and divinely guided in her judgments she proscribes
the books that have evil in them. I glory in the
Church's *Index* of those poisonous books that would
bring peril to her children. If she did not act thus
she could not be the representative of the Good Shep-
herd. The *Index* is not only a protection for the
weak, but it is a logical consequence of the Infallibility of the Church. And the reason why I love it
so much is because the world fears it and hates it so
much. And great need have we to take all care in
these evil days. For now I am certain that infidel-
ity is in the air. Just as a pestilence or an epidemic
comes and we know not why, and men say 'it must
be in the air,' so I am persuaded, as I say, that unbelief is hanging round us, like the very air we
breathe. Our Lord tells us of the time in which no
flesh could be saved, if the days were not shortened;
but He also tells us that for the sake of the elect He
Himself has shortened those days. Now I hate all
half-measures and I for one intend always to take
my stand clearly and definitely on the side of the
Vicar of our Lord. I intend never to temporize with
the world nor to preach any other Gospel but that
which I have received. That Gospel is the message
of the Cross of Christ. I know of no easy ways of
salvation. What are our Lord's Own words? "Enter ye in at the narrow gate; for wide is the gate
and broad is the way that leadeth to destruction, and

many there are who go in thereat. How narrow is
the gate and how strait is the way, that leadeth to
life : and few there are that find it." Very terrible
words are these, and yet very loving words if we
rightly understand them. But who will venture to
tamper with them ? What right have I, what right
has any one, to pare down the requirements of the
Gospel to suit the maxims of the fashionable world
or the money-making world or the world of honor
without religion ? It is by fearlessly confronting
the world and not by flattering it that the world is
to be overcome and destroyed. I would to God that
we had a little of the spirit of the Catacombs in us in
these days. I would to God that all Catholics would
learn to despise the world and to hate it ? But what
do I see ? I see that many of them are timeservers
with much thought about this world and little
thought about the next. I see that many of them
are insincere and worldly and forgetful of God, desirous of standing well with their neighbours, anxious
above all things to get amongst Protestants and
stand well with them. It is this that keeps many
people out of the Church. A person once said to me,
' Why should I be a Catholic ? I have Catholic
friends and they are just as worldly and as fond of
pleasure as myself.' Could anything be more humil-
iating than this ? So the world gets a footing in
the Church ; and draws men away from the thought
of Calvary and the Crown of thorns. This is a woe
and a sorrow ; it is like " the abomination of desol-

like this scheme; and I detest it with all my heart
and soul. But I should be very sorry to say anything disrespectful of those who are out of the Church.
Still I must speak the truth. I wish to live amongst
them in all kindness and charity; but I am deter-
mined to take nothing from them as far as the soul
is concerned. As I disbelieve their theology, so I
distrust their metaphysics. I have no wish to compel any man's belief, for I see that God leaves all
men free to choose between the evil and the good.
Nor should I ever try to do so for I know that it is
impossible. But between them and us there is a
great gulf. They can come to us but we cannot go
to them. It would be eternal death for us to go to
them; but it is eternal life for them to come to us.
I have not and never have had any unkind feelings
about any of them personally, either those whom I
knew or those whom I did not know. Some have
imagined and said that converts are especially bitter
against the sect to which they belonged. This is a
great mistake. To Catholics all sects are the same.
And we have no hatred for persons but only for systems. For myself my heart turns most towards those
persons (chiefly I believe to be found amongst
Wesleyan Methodists) who, blindly indeed and
ignorantly, yet sincerely as far as they know, hold
the doctrines of Grace, and have a real personal
love for our most Holy Redeemer, Jesus Christ.
The sect to which I once belonged seems to me
neither better nor worse on the whole than the rest.

It is better in some things and worse in others. I
have for it neither any particular liking nor any spe-
cial dislike. I simply know that once I was out of
the Church and that now by the grace of God I am
in it. And I mean to stay in it. I also mean to do
what I can for it. I owe nothing whatever to any
sect but all to the grace of God. We all feel in this
matter much I suppose as Abraham, after his
call, felt towards "Ur of the Chaldees." Lutherans,
Wesleyans, Anglicans, Baptists, and Independents,
are simply out of the Church and that is all you can
say. When I see any signs of decay and disorder
in any of these bodies I rejoice greatly, because
I desire greatly that all forms of error should
be destroyed and that the Kingdom and Truth of
God should be triumphant. That Kingdom is the
Roman Church; that Truth is the Catholic Faith.
And yet indeed I feel nothing but sorrow for any
individual soul which goes downward to the darkness; I mourn over it, if it gives up any of its light
or parts with any of its belief. But I feel great joy
when any sect perishes from the face of the earth, or
when it is tending to that end. I grieve for the
cause though I rejoice in the effect, for God brings
good out of evil. And indeed the first thought we
must always have is for the glory of God and the
good of His Church. And thus, although as I said
I have only kindly feelings to individual Protestants
yet of course, if I could, I would hew Protestantism
in pieces this day, before the Blessed Sacrament, as

Samuel hewed Agag in pieces before the Lord in
Galgal. If I did not feel thus I should consider
myself a traitor to the Heavenly King. All forms
of error whether intellectual or moral are alike
hateful. But I look forward to the day of which
our Lord spoke when He said; "Other sheep I
have that are not of this fold; them also I must
bring and there shall be one Fold and One Shep-
herd." Here I may say one word about the unity
of Christendom. That unity now is broken, for un-
fortunately Christendom is not now as it once was
co-extensive with the Church. The Church is
always perfectly one. By Christendom I understand all who profess the name of Christ. Besides
the Roman Church, which is the one true Church of
Jesus Christ, there is the schismatical Greek Church;
there are also many heretical sects, such as I mentioned before, Lutherans, Anglicans, Wesleyans,
with Baptists and Independents, as far as they
keep away from Calvinism. In the widest sense of
the word it seems difficult to apply it to such
sects as Calvinists, Unitarians, or Quakers. Still
in a certain sense we may include even these.
All who truly desire the unity of Christendom ought
to thank God greatly that the Holy Father, in his
ever-watchful care, has so utterly condemned a certain society called "The Association for promoting
the Unity of Christendom." The Vicar of Christ,
speaking by the mouth of the President of the Holy
Inquisition, has declared the intention of that society

to be "as much as possible polluted by heresy;" and
he also tells us that no Catholic can unite himself
with it in any way, and yet "preserve the integrity
of his faith." I never could understand how any
Catholics could have anything to do with it. But
now since the Holy See has spoken, no Catholics
of course can join it or favor it or help it in any
way or under any pretence, unless they are thoroughly disloyal, and manifest the same evasive spirit
as the Jansenists did. And in all brotherly love I
beseech those persons, who may be led astray in this
matter, to consider what they are doing, lest that
which came to the Jansenists may also come to them.
There is no spirit approved by God, but a spirit of
absolute and unconditional submission in every moment to the living voice of the Holy See. Sooner
or later anything but this, if time be given it, must
end in heresy. And indeed if any man is dissatisfied with the Church he can leave the Church, just
as a man who is dissatisfied with God can act accordingly, though I do not pretend to say how that
would be. Men come freely into the Church for the
salvation of their souls, and they can go freely out
of it, if they please, at their own peril. As for me I
can say truly that the Church is far more than ever
I expected her to be. Her theology, dogmatic, moral, ascetical, mystical, is so comprehensive and so
precise, that I literally had, as I now find, no idea
of it whatever. All her ways, her sayings and do-
ings, as I may call them, are far more graceful and

attractive than ever entered into my mind. And she herself, indefectible, infallible, and unchangable, is grander and more majestic than the fairest vision of her power and loveliness of which I ever dreamed.

If any person wants to promote the unity of Christendom let him come into this one Church of God. Then he will have done all he can do to further the great and blessed end which he has at heart. But if any persons think they can further this end by remaining in the sect, whatever it be, to which they belong and by seeking to Catholicize it, then in the words of their own Bible "they are given up to a strong delusion to believe a lie." When will these persons come to see that union with Rome means always submission to Rome? The divine, infallible Church of God can grant no terms but unconditional surrender. The Association of which I speak ought to have been called "The Association for *preventing* the unity of Christendom;" for in so far as it keeps any persons out of the Church it does this. Its ruling spirit is satan transformed into an angel of light. I say this because the unity of Christendom is so good and holy a thing that every one ought to desire it, pray for it, work for it. But there is only one way in which those who are out of the Church can work for this end, and that is by individual submission to the Holy See. If therefore any persons profess to seek for this good end by wrong means, it is clear that they have not with them an angel of light

but an angel of darkness in disguise. But whilst
the Holy Inquisition, so venerable for all the many
blessings it has conferred and does confer on the
Church, gives us such a proof of its watchful care as
it has done in the condemnation of this society, we
cannot fear.

Now I have said all this to show that in opposing
this "Oxford scheme" I have no hard thoughts of
any kind as to individual Protestants. I should be
grieved if any one thought that I had. But with all
my strength I oppose the system by which they are
misled, and with it I can make no truce. The kind-
est thing to do to them is not to pay them idle com-
pliments or court them or flatter them, but to speak
to them "the truth in love." And, blessed be God,
we know the Truth, and the Truth has made us free.
As we want no pattern of an altar from Damascus,
so we need no help in this matter from those who
are out of the Church.

Again therefore I say that I have not written one
word here which could justly give offence to any
Protestant. But it is well for us to have a clear un-
derstanding of our relative positions. I like and
respect a straightforward antagonist who is fair and
above-board in what he says and does. If a man
thoroughly and sincerely thinks me mistaken, I like
him to say so plainly and not mince the matter. And
that which I desire others to be towards me, I desire
to be towards them. Nor have I written a word of
which you can justly complain. Certainly I have not

been able to see any force in your arguments, but I do *not* think I am "probably to blame" for that. I have spoken strongly against this plan for I feel strongly, but I have given you credit for the best motives. I can have no personal feelings in the matter, for I have no more idea now than when I began this letter who you are. But had I known this, it would have made no difference in a single word that I have written.

I will only add this : let us be loyal in every thought to the Holy See, for thus and only thus we shall have God at our backs. And as we love God with a strong, undying love, so let us hate heresy with a strong, undying hatred. If we ever begin to slacken in our hatred of heresy, we may be sure there is something amiss with our souls. Just hatred of heresy is a great gift of God ; and many souls are shipwrecked for want of it.

As for this scheme, let it be hidden in its own darkness ; and " let the dead bury their dead." It is a hateful scheme, " of the earth, earthly." It is contrary to Catholic instincts, and does violence to the conscience of the Church. In metaphysics and philosophy of all kinds we ought to follow the spirit of Rome, and the guidance of the See of St. Peter. False philosophy is the herald of false doctrine.

I am, Sir, Your obedient Servant,

H. A. RAWES.

St. Francis of Assisi, Notting Hill.
Nov. 24th, 1864.

www.ingramcontent.com/pod-product-compliance
Lightning Source LLC
Chambersburg PA
CBHW031453270326
41930CB00007B/985